THE ESSENTIAL ITALIAN COOKBOOK

THE MOST DELICIOUS RECIPES OF THE BEST CUISINE IN THE WORLD

ANTONIO GRANT

TABLE OF CONTENTS:

CHAPTER 1: BREAKFAST RECIPES 7
- ITALIAN BISCOTTI 8
- HAM, BASIL, AND FETA SCRAMBLED EGGS 10
- GARLIC-BUTTER ROASTED MUSHROOMS 12
- ITALIAN ANISE BREAD 14
- BREAKFAST CHEESESTEAKS 17
- BANANA ROLL FRENCH TOAST 19
- FANTASTIC EGG DROP SOUP 21
- TOMATO ORZO SOUP 23
- CHEESY SAUSAGE AND EGG BAKE 25
- AMAZING BRIOCHE 27
- ITALIAN FRITTATA 30
- BREAKFAST STRATA 34
- MINI BREAKFAST QUICHES 37

CHAPTER 2: PASTA RECIPES 40
- PASTA WITH PEAS AND SAUSAGE 41
- PASTA POMODORO 43
- CREAMY SHRIMP PASTA 45
- PASTA WITH ASPARAGUS 47
- PASTA SICILIANO 49
- CREAMY GORGONZOLA SPINACH PASTA 51
- CREAMY PASTA CARBONARA 53
- SPAGHETTI CACIO E PEPE 55
- PESTO SHRIMP PASTA 57

CHAPTER 3: ITALIAN DISHES RECIPES 60
- ITALIAN VEGGIE ROLLS 61
- LASAGNA 64
- LOBSTER TAILS IN CHAMPAGNE 68
- AMAZING FRIED CALAMARI 70
- CARAMELIZED CHICKEN WINGS 80
- NEAPOLITAN-STYLE PIZZA DOUGH WITH GARLIC AND ITALIAN SEASONINGS . 82
- SPICY SLIDERS 85
- MEATLOAF MUFFINS WITH OATS 87

LEMON AND CILANTRO SHRIMP	90
SESAME-ROASTED SALMON	92
GRILLED POTATO SALAD	94
GRILLED COD	96
OYSTERS ROCKEFELLER	98

CHAPTER 4: DESSERT RECIPES 101

LEMON CREAM PIE BARS	102
FANTASTIC STRUFOLI	104
PANNA COTTA	109
LEMON PUDDING CAKE	111

© Copyright 2021 by Antonio Grant All rights reserved.

The following Book is reproduced below with the goal of providing information that is as accurate and reliable as possible. Regardless, purchasing this Book can be seen as consent to the fact that both the publisher and the author of this book are in no way experts on the topics discussed within and that any recommendations or suggestions that are made herein are for entertainment purposes only. Professionals should be consulted as needed prior to undertaking any of the action endorsed herein.

This declaration is deemed fair and valid by both the American Bar Association and the Committee of Publishers Association and is legally binding throughout the United States. Furthermore, the transmission, duplication, or reproduction of any of the following work including specific information will be considered an illegal act irrespective of if it is done electronically or in print. This extends to creating a secondary or tertiary copy of the work or a recorded copy and is only allowed with the express written consent from the Publisher. All additional right reserved.

The information in the following pages is broadly considered a truthful and accurate account of facts and as such, any inattention, use, or misuse of the information in question by the reader will render any resulting actions solely under their purview. There are no scenarios in which the publisher or the original author of this work can be in any fashion deemed liable for any hardship or damages that may befall them after undertaking information described herein.

Additionally, the information in the following pages is intended only for informational purposes and should thus be thought of as universal. As befitting its nature, it is presented without assurance regarding its prolonged validity or interim quality. Trademarks that are mentioned are done without written consent and can in no way be considered an endorsement from the trademark holder.

CHAPTER 1:

BREAKFAST

RECIPES

ITALIAN BISCOTTI

Servings:
30
Yield:
30 cookies

INGREDIENTS:

6 cups all-purpose flour
½ teaspoon salt
2 teaspoons baking powder
8 ounces chopped almonds
12 ounces butter
1 ¾ cups white sugar
6 eggs
1 teaspoon anise extract
2 teaspoons vanilla extract

DIRECTIONS:

1

Preheat oven to 350 degrees F (165 degrees C).

2

In a large bowl, cream the butter and sugar together.
Add eggs one at a time; beat until fluffy.
Stir in the anise
and vanilla extracts.
Sift together the flour,
baking powder, and salt;
Add them to the egg mixture along with the chopped almonds.
Stir with a spoon and as the dough comes together,
Knead by hand.

3

Divide the dough into 4 parts. Roll each
piece into a log about 15 inches long.
Place logs onto cookie sheets, 2 to a sheet, the long way.
 Flatten the logs out until they are about
3 inches wide with a slight hump
going down the middle. Bake for 25 to 30
minutes in the preheated oven, loaves should be firm.
Cut the loaves into diagonal slices 1/2 inch wide, place the slices onto the cookie
sheets and return to the oven.
 Toast on one side, then turn them over to do the other side.
This will take about 7 to 10 minutes.

NUTRITION FACTS:

275 calories; protein 5.5g; carbohydrates 32.4g; fat 14.1g;

HAM, BASIL, AND FETA SCRAMBLED EGGS

Prep:
10 mins
Cook:
5 mins
Total:
15 mins
Servings:
2
Yield:
2 servings

INGREDIENTS:

¼ cup crumbled feta cheese
1 tablespoon dried basil
salt and pepper to taste
4 eggs, lightly beaten
½ cup diced cooked ham
1 ½ teaspoons butter

DIRECTIONS:

1

Place a skillet over medium heat. Place the lightly beaten eggs in a bowl; stir in the ham, feta cheese, basil, salt, and pepper.

2

Melt the butter in the skillet. Pour in the egg mixture; cook and stir eggs until firmed and no longer runny, about 5 minutes.

NUTRITION FACTS:

328 calories; protein 22.7g; carbohydrates 3.4g; fat 25g; cholesterol 424mg;

GARLIC-BUTTER ROASTED MUSHROOMS

Prep:
10 mins
Cook:
20 mins
Total:
30 mins
Servings:
4
Yield:
4 servings

INGREDIENTS:

Original recipe yields 4 servings
Ingredient Checklist
1 pound fresh white mushrooms
1 tablespoon olive oil
2 cloves garlic, minced
3 tablespoons salted butter, melted
1 pinch salt and ground black pepper to taste
2 tablespoons grated Parmesan cheese
2 tablespoons minced fresh parsley

DIRECTIONS:

1

Preheat the oven to 400 degrees F (200 degrees C).

2

Clean mushrooms with a damp paper
towel and gently remove and discard stems.

3

Drizzle oil into a large cast iron skillet to evenly coat.
Place mushrooms into the skillet, cap-side down.
Carefully sprinkle garlic into the mushroom cavities,
taking care not to sprinkle directly into the skillet.
Drizzle mushrooms with melted butter,
then season with salt and pepper.

4

Roast in the preheated oven for 15 minutes.
Sprinkle with Parmesan cheese and return
to the oven for 3 to 5 more minutes.
Remove from the oven and sprinkle with parsley.
Let cool slightly before serving.

NUTRITION FACTS:

145 calories; protein 4.7g; carbohydrates 4.4g; fat 13.1g;

ITALIAN ANISE BREAD

Prep:
15 mins
Cook:
45 mins
Additional:
9 hrs
Total:
10 hrs
Servings:
20
Yield:
6 loaves

INGREDIENTS:

2 (.25 ounce) packages active dry yeast
2 cups warm milk
8 eggs, at room temperature
½ cup butter, melted
12 ⅜ cups all-purpose flour
2 cups white sugar
5 tablespoons anise seed
½ cup warm water

DIRECTIONS:

1
Combine flour, sugar, and anise seed together
in a very large bowl; create a well in the center.

2
Mix warm water and yeast together in a bowl.
Let stand until the yeast softens and begins to form a creamy foam,
about 10 minutes.

3
Beat warm milk, eggs, and butter together in a bowl;
stir into yeast mixture.
 Add milk mixture to the well in the flour mixture.
 Knead flour-milk mixture using
your hands until dough and your hands are no longer sticky.
Cover dough with a clean cotton cloth and let rise,
8 hours to overnight.

4
Grease and flour 6 loaf pans.

5
Punch dough down and divide into 6 portions. Mold each portion into a round shape and
place each in a prepared pan. Cover pans and let rise for 1 hour more.

6
Preheat oven to 350 degrees F (175 degrees C).

7
Bake in the preheated oven until bread is cooked through,
45 to 50 minutes.

NUTRITION FACTS:

448 calories; protein 11.9g; carbohydrates 81.4g; fat 8.1g;

BREAKFAST CHEESESTEAKS

Prep:
5 mins
Cook:
20 mins
Additional:
5 mins
Total:
30 mins
Servings:
2
Yield:
2 servings

INGREDIENTS:

6 large eggs, divided
2 tablespoons milk
4 thick slices bread
1 (5 ounce) package Chicken Sausage Patties
1 tablespoon olive oil
1 clove garlic, minced
½ red bell pepper, thinly sliced
½ green bell pepper, thinly sliced
½ small red onion, thinly sliced
2 slices provolone cheese
Salt and pepper, to taste

DIRECTIONS:

1
In medium bowl, whisk together 2 eggs and milk;
dip bread into egg mixture until fully coated.
Cook French toast on griddle or large skillet
over medium heat until golden brown on both sides.

2
Cook sausage patties according to package instructions.
Cut into strips.

3
In separate skillet, heat olive oil over medium heat.
Add garlic, peppers and onions and
saute until browned and tender.

4
Add cooked sausage strips to pepper and onion mixture;
top with cheese and heat until cheese is melted.

5
Cook remaining eggs over easy, or as desired.

6
Assemble cheesesteaks by layering french toast with eggs,
and pepper, sausage and cheese mixture.
Season with salt & pepper and serve open-faced.

NUTRITION FACTS:

667 calories; protein 44.2g; carbohydrates 38.1g; fat 37.7g;

BANANA ROLL FRENCH TOAST

Prep:
15 mins
Cook:
10 mins
Total:
25 mins
Servings:
8
Yield:
8 servings

INGREDIENTS:

2 teaspoons vegetable oil
8 large slices whole wheat bread
2 bananas, mashed
1 (8 ounce) package cream cheese, softened
2 tablespoons white sugar
¼ teaspoon ground cinnamon
2 eggs

DIRECTIONS:

1
Heat oil in a skillet over medium heat.

2
Flatten bread slices using a rolling pin.
Mix bananas
and cream cheese together in a bowl; add sugar
and cinnamon and mix well. Whisk eggs in a separate bowl.

3
Spread about 2 1/2 tablespoons banana mixture
onto 1 end of each flattened bread slice. Roll bread slice around filling.
Dip bread rolls in the egg until coated
and place in the hot skillet,
working in batches if needed.

4
Cook French toast rolls in the hot oil until browned,
2 to 3 minutes per side. Repeat with remaining rolls.

NUTRITION FACTS:

234 calories; protein 7.7g; carbohydrates 22.5g; fat 13.2g;

FANTASTIC EGG DROP SOUP

Servings:
4
Yield:
4 servings

INGREDIENTS:

1 teaspoon dried parsley
1 tablespoon dried minced onion
1 tablespoon cornstarch
4 cups water
4 cubes chicken bouillon
2 eggs

DIRECTIONS:

1
In a medium saucepan, combine water, bouillon,
and parsley and onion flakes. Bring to a boil.

2
Lightly beat eggs together. Gradually stir into soup.

3
Remove about half a cup of the soup.
Stir in cornstarch until there are no lumps,
and return to the soup.
 Boil until soup thickens.

NUTRITION FACTS:

56 calories; protein 4g; carbohydrates 3.9g; fat 2.7g;

TOMATO ORZO SOUP

Prep:
10 mins
Cook:
30 mins
Total:
40 mins
Servings:
8
Yield:
8 servings

INGREDIENTS:

7 ½ cups water
2 (10.5 ounce) cans vegetable broth
2 (10.75 ounce) cans condensed tomato soup
5 teaspoons chicken bouillon powder
1 ½ cups diced carrots
1 ½ cups diced celery
1 cup green peas
1 ½ cups uncooked orzo pasta
½ cup fresh parsley

DIRECTIONS:

1

Place water, chicken broth, tomato soup,
chicken bouillon, carrots, celery,
peas and orzo pasta in large stock pot and bring to boil.
Reduce heat and simmer for 30 minutes,
or until vegetables are tender.
Sprinkle with parsley just before serving.

NUTRITION FACTS:

251 calories; protein 9.3g; carbohydrates 49.4g;
fat 2.4g; cholesterol 0.8mg;

CHEESY SAUSAGE AND EGG BAKE

Prep:
25 mins
Cook:
35 mins
Total:
1 hr
Servings:
12
Yield:
12 servings

INGREDIENTS:

- 1 pound bulk pork sausage, cooked and drained
- 1 ½ cups sliced fresh mushrooms
- 8 medium green onions, sliced
- 2 medium tomatoes, seeded and chopped
- 2 cups shredded mozzarella cheese
- 1 ¼ cups Bisquick mix
- 1 cup milk
- 1 ½ teaspoons salt
- 1 ½ tablespoons chopped fresh oregano
- ½ teaspoon ground black pepper
- 12 large eggs eggs

DIRECTIONS:

1
Heat oven to 350 degrees F. Grease rectangular baking dish,
13x9x2 inches. Layer sausage, mushrooms,
onions, tomatoes and cheese in dish.

2
Stir remaining ingredients until blended. Pour over cheese.

3
Bake uncovered 30 to 35 minutes or until golden brown and set.

NUTRITION FACTS:

286 calories; protein 18.2g; carbohydrates 11.8g;
fat 18.5g; cholesterol 221.3mg;

AMAZING BRIOCHE

Prep:
40 mins
Cook:
30 mins
Additional:
1 day
Total:
1 day
Servings:
16
Yield:
2 9x5-inch loaves

INGREDIENTS:

4 eggs
1 cup butter, softened
1 egg yolk
1 tablespoon active dry yeast
⅓ cup warm water (110 degrees F)
3 ½ cups all-purpose flour
1 tablespoon white sugar
1 teaspoon salt
1 teaspoon cold water

DIRECTIONS:

1

In a small bowl, dissolve yeast in warm water.
Let stand until creamy, about 10 minutes.

2

In a large bowl, stir together the flour sugar and salt.
Make a well in center of the bowl
and mix in the eggs and yeast mixture.
Beat well until the dough has pulled together,
then turn it out onto a lightly floured surface
and knead until smooth and supple, about 8 minutes.

3

Flatten the dough and spread it with
 one third of the butter.
Knead this well. Repeat this twice to incorporate
the remaining butter.
Allow the dough to rest for a few minutes
between additions of butter.
This process may take 20 minutes or so.
Lightly oil a large bowl,
place the dough in the bowl and turn to coat with oil.
Cover with plastic wrap and let rise in
a warm place until doubled in volume, about 1 hour.

4

Deflate the dough,
cover with plastic wrap,
 and refrigerate 6
hours or overnight. It needs time to chill
in order to become more workable.

5
Turn the dough out onto
a lightly floured surface.
 Divide the dough into
two equal pieces,
 form into loaves and place
 into prepared pans.
 Cover with greased plastic wrap and
let rise until doubled in volume,
about 60 minutes.

6
Preheat oven to 400 degrees F (200 degrees C).
 Lightly grease two 9x5-inch loaf pans
(see Cook's Note to make rolls). Beat the egg yolk
with 1 teaspoon of water to make a glaze.

7
Brush the loaves or rolls with the egg wash.
 Bake in preheated oven until a
deep golden brown.
Start checking the loaves for doneness after 25 minutes,
and rolls at 10 minutes.
Let the loaves cool in the pans for 10 minutes
 before moving them to wire racks to cool completely.

NUTRITION FACTS:

228 calories; protein 5g; carbohydrates 22.1g; fat 13.3g;

ITALIAN FRITTATA

Prep:
25 mins
Cook:
25 mins
Total:
50 mins
Servings:
6
Yield:
6 servings

INGREDIENTS:

½ cup diced salami
½ cup artichoke hearts, drained and chopped
½ cup chopped cherry tomatoes
1 (4.5 ounce) can sliced mushrooms, drained
1 teaspoon salt
ground black pepper to taste
⅓ cup grated Parmesan cheese
1 cup shredded mozzarella cheese
6 eggs
⅓ cup milk
2 green onions, chopped
1 clove garlic, minced
1 teaspoon dried basil
1 teaspoon onion powder

DIRECTIONS:

1
Preheat oven to 425 degrees F (220 degrees C).
Grease a shallow 2-quart baking dish.

2
Heat a skillet over medium heat; cook and stir salami,
 artichokes, tomatoes, and mushrooms until heated through,
about 4 minutes.
 Transfer salami mixture to baking dish.

3
Whisk eggs, milk, green onions,
 garlic, basil, onion powder, salt, and black
pepper in a large bowl; pour eggs over salami mixture.
 Sprinkle with mozzarella cheese and Parmesan cheese.

4
Bake until eggs are set and cheese is melted,
 about 20 minutes.

NUTRITION FACTS:

211 calories; protein 17g; carbohydrates 5.9g; fat 13.4g;

POTATO AND PEPPER FRITTATA

Prep:
20 mins
Cook:
20 mins
Total:
40 mins
Servings:
4
Yield:
4 servings

INGREDIENTS:

6 slices bacon or pancetta, chopped
1 tablespoon olive oil
1 ½ cups chopped hot and sweet peppers
salt and ground black pepper to taste
½ teaspoon red pepper flakes, or more to taste
1 ½ cups cubed cooked potatoes
12 eggs, beaten
2 ounces crumbled feta cheese

DIRECTIONS:

1
Place bacon and olive oil in a large skillet
over medium heat. Cook until bacon is nearly crisp,
5 to 7 minutes.
Add peppers; cook and stir over
medium heat until softened,
about 3 minutes. Remove from heat and drain
excess grease from the pan. Season with salt,
black pepper, and red pepper flakes; stir to combine.

2
Return pan to medium heat, add potatoes and
stir until warmed through, about 2 minutes.
Pour in eggs and slowly stir to form large,
soft curds, about 5 minutes.
Sprinkle feta cheese over
the top and stir gently to incorporate.

3
Set oven rack about 6 inches from
the heat source and preheat the oven's broiler.

4
Place pan under the preheated broiler
and cook until the top is set and
feta cheese is browned, about 5 minutes.

NUTRITION FACTS:

434 calories; protein 28.3g; carbohydrates 20g;
fat 27.3g; cholesterol 585.7mg;

BREAKFAST STRATA

Prep:
20 mins
Cook:
1 hr 15 mins
Additional:
2 hrs
Total:
3 hrs 35 mins
Servings:
8
Yield:
8 serving

INGREDIENTS:

1 pound sausage, casings removed
2 cups sliced fresh mushrooms
8 eggs, beaten
10 cups cubed, day-old bread
3 cups whole milk
2 cups shredded Cheddar cheese
1 ½ cups cubed Black Forest ham
1 (10 ounce) package frozen chopped spinach, thawed and drained
2 tablespoons all-purpose flour
2 tablespoons mustard powder
1 teaspoon salt
2 teaspoons butter, melted
2 teaspoons dried basil

DIRECTIONS:

1
Generously grease a 9x13-inch casserole dish.

2
Heat a skillet over medium heat; cook and stir
sausage until crumbly and completely browned,
about 10 minutes.
Transfer cooked sausage to the prepared casserole dish.

3
Cook and stir mushrooms in the same skillet
over medium heat until liquid has been released
and mushrooms are lightly browned, 5 to 10 minutes; drain.

4
Mix mushrooms, eggs, bread, milk,
Cheddar cheese, ham, spinach, flour,
mustard powder, salt, butter,
and basil together in a large bowl;
pour over sausage.
Cover casserole dish and refrigerate, 2 hours to overnight.

5
Preheat oven to 350 degrees F (175 degrees C).

6
Bake in the preheated oven until a knife
inserted into the center of the strata comes
out clean, 60 to 70 minutes.

NUTRITION FACTS:

600 calories; protein 34.2g; carbohydrates 32g; fat 37.2g;

MINI BREAKFAST QUICHES

Prep:
20 mins
Cook:
30 mins
Total:
50 mins
Servings:
12
Yield:
24 mini quiches

INGREDIENTS:

24 (2 inch) frozen mini tart shells
6 slices bacon
½ cup diced red bell pepper
½ cup cubed fully cooked ham
¼ cup salsa
½ cup shredded Cheddar cheese
6 eggs
1 ½ cups heavy cream
¼ cup all-purpose flour
2 teaspoons garlic salt
2 teaspoons onion powder
1 teaspoon chili powder
½ teaspoon ground cumin
2 cups shredded Cheddar cheese
½ cup diced green bell pepper

DIRECTIONS:

1
Preheat an oven to 375 degrees F
(190 degrees C). Place the tart shells
into muffin pans and set aside.

2
Cook the bacon in a large, deep skillet over
medium-high heat, turning occasionally,
until evenly browned, about 10 minutes.
Drain on a paper towel-lined plate; crumble once cool.

3
Beat the eggs in a mixing bowl; whisk in the cream,
flour, garlic salt, onion powder, chili powder,
and cumin until smooth. Stir in the crumbled bacon,
2 cups Cheddar cheese, green bell pepper,
red bell pepper, ham, and salsa.
Ladle the mixture into the tart shells;
sprinkle with 1/2 cup of Cheddar cheese.

4
Bake in the preheated
oven until a knife inserted
into the center of the quiche comes out clean,
20 to 25 minutes.

NUTRITION FACTS:

545 calories; protein 16.2g;
carbohydrates 35.3g; fat 37.7g;

CHAPTER 2: PASTA RECIPES

PASTA WITH PEAS AND SAUSAGE

Prep:
15 mins
Cook:
10 mins
Total:
25 mins
Servings:
8
Yield:
8 servings

INGREDIENTS:

1 pound rigatoni pasta
2 tablespoons olive oil
1 clove garlic, minced
1 pound sweet Italian sausage, casings removed
12 ounces frozen green peas
1 ½ cups heavy cream
4 tablespoons butter
2 tablespoons grated Parmesan cheese

DIRECTIONS:

1

Bring a large pot of lightly salted water to a boil. Add pasta and cook for 8 to 10 minutes or until al dente; drain.

2

In a skillet heat oil and saute garlic over medium heat. Brown sausage in skillet. Once brown add frozen peas and simmer for 5 minutes. Slowly add heavy cream and butter to skillet; bring to a slight boil. Add more cream if necessary. Cook for 5 minutes. Toss with cooked pasta and top with Parmesan cheese.

NUTRITION FACTS:

611 calories; protein 18.7g; carbohydrates 50.2g; fat 38.2g; cholesterol 99.8mg; sodium 599.3mg.

PASTA POMODORO

Prep:
15 mins
Cook:
15 mins
Total:
30 mins
Servings:
4
Yield:
4 servings

INGREDIENTS:

1 (16 ounce) package angel hair pasta
¼ cup olive oil
½ onion, chopped
4 cloves garlic, minced
2 cups roma (plum) tomatoes, diced
2 tablespoons balsamic vinegar
1 (10.75 ounce) can low-sodium chicken broth
crushed red pepper to taste
freshly ground black pepper to taste
2 tablespoons chopped fresh basil
¼ cup grated Parmesan cheese

DIRECTIONS:

1
Bring a large pot of lightly salted water to a boil. Add pasta and cook for 8 minutes or until al dente; drain.

2
Pour olive oil in a large deep skillet over high-heat. Saute onions and garlic until lightly browned. Reduce heat to medium-high and add tomatoes, vinegar and chicken broth; simmer for about 8 minutes.

3
Stir in red pepper, black pepper, basil and cooked pasta, tossing thoroughly with sauce. Simmer for about 5 more minutes and serve topped with grated cheese.

NUTRITION FACTS:

500 calories; protein 16.2g; carbohydrates 69.7g; fat 18.3g; cholesterol 5.7mg; sodium 349.9mg.

CREAMY SHRIMP PASTA

Prep:
10 mins
Cook:
15 mins
Total:
25 mins
Servings:
4
Yield:
4 servings

INGREDIENTS:

1 (16 ounce) package spaghetti
1 tablespoon olive oil
2 cloves garlic, minced
1 ¼ pounds shrimp, peeled and deveined
1 splash dry white wine
1 cup heavy whipping cream
¼ cup chopped fresh basil
salt and freshly ground black pepper to taste
1 tablespoon grated Parmesan cheese

DIRECTIONS:

1
Bring a large pot of lightly salted water to a boil. Cook spaghetti in the boiling water, stirring occasionally, until tender yet firm to the bite, about 12 minutes.

2
While spaghetti is cooking, heat oil in a large skillet over medium heat. Cook garlic until soft, but not brown, about 1 minute. Add shrimp and cook until opaque, about 3 minutes. Add wine, reduce heat, and pour in cream. Simmer until sauce starts to thicken, 3 to 5 minutes. Stir in basil and season with salt and pepper.

3
Drain spaghetti and spoon creamy shrimp on top. Serve with Parmesan cheese.

NUTRITION FACTS:

780 calories; protein 39.7g; carbohydrates 86.3g; fat 28.7g; cholesterol 298.6mg; sodium 336.4mg.

PASTA WITH ASPARAGUS

Prep:
15 mins
Cook:
10 mins
Total:
25 mins
Servings:
4
Yield:
4 servings

INGREDIENTS:

1 ½ pounds fresh asparagus, trimmed and cut into 1 inch pieces
¼ cup chicken broth
½ pound fresh mushrooms, sliced
8 ounces angel hair pasta
1 tablespoon olive oil
½ teaspoon crushed red pepper
½ cup grated Parmesan cheese

DIRECTIONS:

1
Cook pasta according to package instructions.

2
Heat the olive oil in a nonstick skillet. Saute asparagus in the pan over medium heat for about 3 minutes. Add chicken broth and mushroom slices; cook 3 minutes more.

3
Drain pasta, and transfer to a serving dish. Gently toss pasta with asparagus mixture; sprinkle with Parmesan and crushed red pepper.

NUTRITION FACTS:

281 calories; protein 15.5g; carbohydrates 39.4g; fat 8.4g; cholesterol 8.8mg; sodium 338.6mg.

PASTA SICILIANO

Prep:
15 mins
Cook:
20 mins
Total:
35 mins
Servings:
8
Yield:
8 servings

INGREDIENTS:

1 (16 ounce) package uncooked farfalle pasta
¼ cup olive oil
3 cloves chopped garlic
1 teaspoon crushed red pepper flakes
2 tablespoons lemon juice
½ cup pine nuts
1 (2.25 ounce) can sliced black olives
½ cup chopped sun-dried tomatoes
1 cup crumbled feta cheese
salt and pepper to taste

DIRECTIONS:

1

Bring a large pot of lightly salted water to a boil. Place farfalle pasta in the pot, cook for 8 to 10 minutes, until al dente, and drain.

2

Heat the oil in a large skillet over medium heat, and cook the garlic until lightly browned. Mix in red pepper and lemon juice. Stir in the pine nuts, olives, and sun-dried tomatoes. Toss in the cooked pasta and feta cheese. Season with salt and pepper.

NUTRITION FACTS:

434 calories; protein 15.3g; carbohydrates 49g; fat 20.1g; cholesterol 28mg; sodium 638.5mg

CREAMY GORGONZOLA SPINACH PASTA

Prep:
5 mins
Cook:
15 mins
Total:
20 mins
Servings:
4
Yield:
4 servings

INGREDIENTS:

1 (16 ounce) package fusilli pasta
1 ½ tablespoons butter
2 shallots, minced
1 cup heavy whipping cream
4 cups fresh spinach
½ cup Gorgonzola cheese
salt and freshly ground black pepper to taste

DIRECTIONS:

1
Bring a large pot of lightly salted water to a boil. Cook fusilli in the boiling water, stirring occasionally, until tender yet firm to the bite, about 12 minutes.

2
In the meantime, melt butter in a skillet over medium heat and cook shallots until soft and translucent, 3 to 5 minutes. Pour in cream and cook until heated through, 3 to 5 minutes. Add spinach and crumble in Gorgonzola cheese. Season with salt and pepper and cook until spinach is wilted and sauce has thickened, about 4 minutes.

3
Drain fusilli and toss with sauce. Serve immediately.

NUTRITION FACTS:

730 calories; protein 21.3g; carbohydrates 88.5g; fat 33.9g; cholesterol 111mg; sodium 293.3mg.

CREAMY PASTA CARBONARA

Prep:
15 mins
Cook:
25 mins
Total:
40 mins
Servings:
4
Yield:
4 servings

INGREDIENTS:

3 cups rigatoni pasta
6 slices bacon, diced
2 cloves garlic, minced
1 ¼ cups milk
1 (8 ounce) package cream cheese, cut into cubes
½ cup butter, softened
½ cup freshly shredded Parmesan cheese
¼ cup fresh green peas
¼ cup diced cooked ham

DIRECTIONS:

1

Bring a large pot of lightly salted water to a boil. Cook rigatoni in the boiling water, stirring occasionally until cooked through but firm to the bite, about 13 minutes. Drain.

2

Meanwhile, place bacon in a large skillet and cook over medium-high heat, turning occasionally, until evenly browned, about 10 minutes. Remove bacon with a slotted spoon, leaving drippings in pan; set bacon aside.

3

Cook and stir garlic in the remaining bacon grease over medium heat. Add milk, cream cheese, and butter to skillet; stir until smooth. Stir Parmesan cheese, peas, ham, and bacon into cream cheese mixture; cook until peas are heated through, about 5 minutes more. Mix pasta into sauce to serve.

NUTRITION FACTS:

778 calories; protein 25.3g; carbohydrates 46.7g; fat 55.5g; cholesterol 156mg; sodium 975.4mg.

SPAGHETTI CACIO E PEPE

Prep:
5 mins
Cook:
18 mins
Total:
23 mins
Servings:
4

INGREDIENTS:

1 pound spaghetti
6 tablespoons olive oil
2 cloves garlic, minced
2 teaspoons ground black pepper
1 ¾ cups grated Pecorino Romano cheese

DIRECTIONS:

1
Bring a large pot of lightly salted water to a boil. Cook spaghetti in the boiling water, stirring occasionally until tender yet firm to the bite, about 10 minutes. Scoop out some of the cooking water and reserve. Drain spaghetti.

2
Heat oil in a large skillet over medium heat. Add garlic and pepper; cook and stir until fragrant, 1 to 2 minutes. Add spaghetti and Pecorino Romano cheese. Ladle in 1/2 cup of reserved cooking water;

stir until cheese is melted, about 1 minute. Add more cooking water until sauce coats spaghetti, about 1 minute more.

NUTRITION FACTS:

807 calories; protein 31.6g; carbohydrates 87.8g; fat 36g; cholesterol 54.1mg; sodium 632.7mg.

PESTO SHRIMP PASTA

Prep:
15 mins
Cook:
25 mins
Total:
40 mins
Servings:
6
Yield:
6 servings

INGREDIENTS:

1 (8 ounce) package spaghetti
1 cup fresh basil leaves
¼ cup lemon juice
3 tablespoons olive oil
1 clove garlic, or to taste
½ teaspoon salt
2 teaspoons olive oil
1 (8 ounce) package sugar snap peas
¾ pound peeled and deveined shrimp
⅛ teaspoon crushed red pepper

DIRECTIONS:

1
Bring a large pot of lightly salted water to a boil. Cook spaghetti in the boiling water, stirring occasionally until cooked through but firm to the bite, about 12 minutes; drain.

2
Blend basil, lemon juice, 3 tablespoons olive oil, garlic, and salt in a blender until smooth.

3
Heat 2 teaspoons olive oil in a skillet over medium heat. Cook and stir sugar snap peas in hot oil until tender, about 5 minutes. Add shrimp and red pepper; continue to cook until the shrimp are bright pink on the outside and the meat is no longer transparent in the center, about 5 minutes. Stir basil sauce into the shrimp mixture and remove from heat; spoon over spaghetti to serve.

NUTRITION FACTS:

279 calories; protein 15.3g; carbohydrates 32.3g; fat 9.4g; cholesterol 86.1mg; sodium 295.6mg.

Antonio Grant

CHAPTER 3: ITALIAN DISHES RECIPES

ITALIAN VEGGIE ROLLS

Prep:
1 hr
Cook:
45 mins
Total:
1 hr 45 mins
Servings:
5
Yield:
4 to 6 servings

INGREDIENTS:

1 cup chopped mushrooms
1 onion, chopped
1 cup sliced carrots
1 cup green peas
1 egg
2 tablespoons olive oil
¼ cup grated Parmesan cheese
1 (16 ounce) package lasagna noodles
1 (26 ounce) jar spaghetti sauce
1 cup chopped broccoli
1 clove garlic, minced
¼ cup dry red wine
2 cups shredded mozzarella cheese

DIRECTIONS:

1
Cook noodles in a large pot of boiling water until
al dente. Rinse,
drain, set aside.

2
Heat oil in a medium saute pan.
 Add mushrooms, onions, carrots, peas, and broccoli;
saute over medium heat until tender.
 Add wine and garlic; cook five minutes,
or until wine has just about evaporated.
Remove from heat, and cool for ten minutes.

3
In a medium bowl combine sauteed vegetable mixture,
mozzarella cheese,
 2 tablespoons Parmesan cheese, and egg. Mix well.

4
Pour half of the sauce into the bottom of a 13x9x2inch baking pan. Spread 1/3 cup vegetable mixture over each lasagna noodle then carefully roll up the noodle. Place seam side down in dish. When finished placing all the noodles in the pan, pour remaining pasta sauce evenly over noodles. Cover with aluminum foil.

5
Bake at 375 degrees F (190 degrees C)
for 35 to 40 minutes. Uncover, and sprinkle remaining
 Parmesan cheese over noodles. Bake, uncovered,
5 more minutes. Garnish and serve immediately.

NUTRITION FACTS:

723 calories; protein 30.2g; carbohydrates 97.1g; fat 23.8g;

LASAGNA

Prep:
1 hr
Cook:
2 hrs
Additional:
10 mins
Total:
3 hrs 10 mins
Servings:
12
Yield:
1 9x13-inch pan

INGREDIENTS:

Sauce:

¼ cup olive oil
1 onion, chopped
1 bay leaf
2 cloves garlic, chopped
2 teaspoons dried oregano
2 teaspoons dried basil
1 (14.5 ounce) can crushed tomatoes
1 (29 ounce) can diced tomatoes
1 pinch ground cinnamon
1 (16 ounce) package lasagna noodles

Cheese Filling:

1 pint part-skim ricotta cheese
2 eggs, beaten
½ cup grated Parmesan cheese
2 teaspoons dried basil
1 clove garlic, minced

Vegetable Filling:

2 tablespoons olive oil
1 onion, sliced
1 pound fresh mushrooms, sliced
1 pound spinach, rinsed and chopped
2 medium zucchini, sliced
1 pound mozzarella cheese, sliced
1 cup grated Parmesan cheese

DIRECTIONS:

1
Heat 1/4 cup oil in a large skillet over medium heat.
Stir in chopped onions and bay leaf;
cook and stir until the onion has softened
and turned translucent, about 5 minutes.
Add 2 cloves minced garlic, oregano, and 2 teaspoons basil;
cook and stir for 2 more minutes.

2
Mix in undrained crushed tomatoes and diced tomatoes.
Bring to a boil, reduce heat,
and simmer for 1 hour.
Stir in cinnamon and set pan aside.

3
Preheat oven to 350 degrees F (175 degrees C).
Lightly grease a 9x13-inch baking dish.

4
Bring a large pot of salted water to boil, add lasagna
noodles and bring water to boil again.
Cook until noodles are al dente. Drain well.

5
Mix together ricotta, eggs, 1/2 cup Parmesan cheese,
2 teaspoons basil, and 1 clove minced garlic.

6
Saute sliced onion and mushrooms
in 2 tablespoons olive oil until tender, about 5 minutes.
Add spinach and zucchini to the skillet.
Cover, and cook until spinach is wilted, 2 to 5 minutes.
Remove skillet from heat and set aside.

7
Spread 1/2 cup of the tomato sauce in the prepared baking dish.
Place a layer of noodles on top of the tomato sauce;
spread all of the ricotta mixture onto the noodles.
Place another layer of noodles on top of the ricotta mixture.

8
Pour about 2 cups tomato sauce onto the noodles;
arrange all of the sauteed vegetables on top of the sauce.
Top vegetables with noodles and spread
the remaining tomato sauce over the final layer of noodles.
Top with mozzarella cheese slices
and 1 cup grated Parmesan cheese.

9
Bake the lasagna in the preheated oven
until filling is bubbly and cheese is melted
and beginning to brown,
 45 minutes to 1 hour.
Remove the lasagna from the oven and
let it cool 10 minutes before serving.

NUTRITION FACTS:

466 calories; protein 28.5g;
carbohydrates 41.9g; fat 21.5g;

LOBSTER TAILS IN CHAMPAGNE

Prep:
10 mins
Cook:
20 mins
Total:
30 mins
Servings:
2
Yield:
2 servings

INGREDIENTS:

⅔ cup Champagne
2 green onions, minced
¼ teaspoon salt
¼ cup heavy whipping cream
¼ stick unsalted butter, cut into tablespoons
2 (8 ounce) frozen lobster tails, rinsed

DIRECTIONS:

1
Combine lobster tails, champagne, green onions, and salt in a skillet; bring to a boil. Reduce heat to medium-low, cover the skillet, and simmer until lobster is cooked through, about 15 minutes. Transfer lobster to a plate.

2
Stir cream in champagne sauce in skillet. Bring to a boil and cook until sauce is reduced to about 1/3 cup, 5 to 10 minutes.

3
Whisk butter into champagne sauce, 1 tablespoon at a time, until sauce is smooth. Cover the skillet and remove from heat.

4
Remove lobsters tails from shells and slice into medallions. Spoon champagne sauce over lobster medallions.

NUTRITION FACTS:

482 calories; protein 35.8g;
carbohydrates 6.4g; fat 27.8g;

AMAZING FRIED CALAMARI

Prep:
15 mins
Cook:
10 mins
Total:
25 mins
Servings:
8
Yield:
8 servings

INGREDIENTS:

1 teaspoon salt
1 teaspoon finely ground black pepper
½ teaspoon cayenne pepper (Optional)
1 tablespoon fresh parsley, or to taste
1 wedge lemon
1 pound calamari tubes, thawed if frozen
peanut oil for frying
6 cups all-purpose flour
2 cups whole milk
4 eggs
1 tablespoon cornstarch (Optional)
1 tablespoon paprika

DIRECTIONS:

1

Check calamari for breaks and slice into 1/8- to 1/4-inch rings.

2

Heat oil in a deep-fryer or large saucepan to 400 degrees F (200 degrees C).

3

Place 2 cups flour in a bowl.
Whisk milk and eggs together in a separate bowl.
Place remaining 4 cups flour, cornstarch, paprika, salt, pepper, and cayenne in a third bowl;
mix thoroughly.

4

Toss calamari rings in the plain flour.
Move to the egg mixture and thoroughly coat.
Move to the seasoned flour and coat fully.
Move back to egg mixture if not thoroughly coated; coat with seasoned flour again.

5

Submerge floured calamari in the hot oil until golden, 3 to 4 minutes per batch. Lift out with a slotted spoon, letting oil drip off. Drain on paper towels.
Place calamari in a small bowl;
check seasoning.
Add parsley and lemon wedge for garnish.

NUTRITION FACTS:

523 calories; protein 22.9g; carbohydrates 79.8g; fat 11.6g;

CHICKEN PARMESAN

Prep:
25 mins
Cook:
20 mins
Additional:
15 mins
Total:
1 hr
Servings:
4
Yield:
4 servings

INGREDIENTS:

4 skinless, boneless chicken breast halves
salt and freshly ground black pepper to taste
¼ cup fresh mozzarella, cut into small cubes
¼ cup chopped fresh basil
½ cup grated provolone cheese
¼ cup grated Parmesan cheese
1 tablespoon olive oil
2 eggs
1 cup panko bread crumbs, or more as needed
½ cup grated Parmesan cheese
2 tablespoons all-purpose flour, or more if needed
1 cup olive oil for frying
½ cup prepared tomato sauce

DIRECTIONS:

1
Preheat an oven to 450 degrees F (230 degrees C).

2
Place chicken breasts between two sheets of heavy plastic (resealable freezer bags work well) on a solid, level surface. Firmly pound chicken with the smooth side of a meat mallet to a thickness of 1/2-inch. Season chicken thoroughly with salt and pepper.

3
Beat eggs in a shallow bowl and set aside.

4
Mix bread crumbs and 1/2 cup Parmesan cheese in a separate bowl, set aside.

5
Place flour in a sifter or strainer; sprinkle over chicken breasts, evenly coating both sides.

6
Dip flour coated chicken breast in beaten eggs. Transfer breast to breadcrumb mixture, pressing the crumbs into both sides. Repeat for each breast. Set aside breaded chicken breasts for about 15 minutes.

7

Heat 1 cup olive oil in a large skillet
on medium-high heat until it begins to shimmer.
Cook chicken until golden,
about 2 minutes on each side.
The chicken will finish cooking in the oven.

8

Place chicken in a baking
dish and top
each breast with about 1/3 cup of tomato sauce.
Layer each chicken breast with equal amounts of mozzarella
cheese, fresh basil, and provolone cheese.
Sprinkle 1 to 2 tablespoons of Parmesan cheese
on top and drizzle
with 1 tablespoon olive oil.

9

Bake in the preheated oven
until cheese is browned and bubbly,
and chicken breasts
are no longer pink in the center,
15 to 20 minutes. An instant-read thermometer
inserted into the center should
read at least 165 degrees F (74 degrees C).

NUTRITION FACTS:

471 calories; protein 42.1g; carbohydrates 24.8g; fat 24.9g;

PESTO CHICKEN

Prep:
10 mins
Cook:
25 mins
Total:
35 mins
Servings:
4
Yield:
4 servings

INGREDIENTS:

4 skinless, boneless chicken breast halves
½ cup prepared basil pesto, divided
4 thin slices prosciutto, or more if needed

DIRECTIONS:

1

Preheat oven to 400 degrees F (200 degrees C). Grease a baking dish.

2

Spread about 2 tablespoons of pesto per chicken breast over the top of each breast, and wrap each breast in prosciutto slices to cover the entire breast. Place the wrapped chicken breasts into the prepared baking dish.

3

Bake in the preheated oven until the chicken is no longer pink, the juices run clear, and the prosciutto is lightly crisped, about 25 minutes.

NUTRITION FACTS:

312 calories; protein 31.5g; carbohydrates 2g; fat 19.3g;

CHICKEN MARSALA

Prep:
15 mins
Cook:
25 mins
Total:
40 mins
Servings:
4
Yield:
4 servings

INGREDIENTS:

¼ cup chopped green onion
1 cup sliced fresh mushrooms
⅓ cup Marsala wine
salt and pepper to taste
⅓ cup heavy cream
1 tablespoon olive oil or vegetable oil
4 skinless, boneless chicken breast halves
⅛ cup milk

DIRECTIONS:

1
Heat oil in a large skilled over medium heat.
Add chicken and saute for 15 to 20 minutes,
or until cooked through and juices run clear.

2
Add green onion and mushrooms
and saute until soft,
then add Marsala
wine and bring to a boil.

3
Boil for 2 to 4 minutes,
seasoning with salt and pepper to taste.
Stir in cream and milk and simmer until heated through,
about 5 minutes.

NUTRITION FACTS:

241 calories; protein 28.4g; carbohydrates 4.9g; fat 9g;

CARAMELIZED CHICKEN WINGS

Prep:
5 mins
Cook:
1 hr
Total:
1 hr 5 mins
Servings:
6
Yield:
12 wings

INGREDIENTS:

1 cup water
½ cup white sugar
⅓ cup soy sauce
2 tablespoons peanut butter
1 tablespoon honey
2 teaspoons wine vinegar
1 tablespoon minced garlic
12 large chicken wings, tips removed and wings cut in half at joint
1 teaspoon sesame seeds, or to taste (Optional)

DIRECTIONS:

1

In an electric skillet or a large skillet over medium heat,
mix together the water, sugar, soy sauce,
peanut butter, honey, wine vinegar,
and garlic until smooth and the sugar has dissolved.
Place the wings into the sauce,
cover, and simmer for 30 minutes.
Uncover and simmer until the wings are tender
and the sauce has thickened,
about 30 more minutes,
spooning sauce over wings occasionally.
Sprinkle with sesame seeds.

NUTRITION FACTS:

529 calories; protein 36.2g; carbohydrates 22.4g;
fat 32.4g; cholesterol 141.7mg;

NEAPOLITAN-STYLE PIZZA DOUGH WITH GARLIC AND ITALIAN SEASONINGS

Prep:
30 mins
Cook:
5 mins
Additional:
1 hr 10 mins
Total:
1 hr 45 mins
Servings:
12
Yield:
2 12-inch crusts

INGREDIENTS:

3 cups unbleached all-purpose flour or as needed
1 ¼ teaspoons salt
½ teaspoon fast-rising dry yeast
1 ½ cups ice water, or as needed
2 tablespoons olive oil
1 tablespoon granulated garlic
1 tablespoon Italian seasoning
½ teaspoon olive oil

DIRECTIONS:

1

In a large bowl, mix the flour, salt, and yeast until thoroughly combined. Mix in ice water, scraping the bowl as you mix, until all the flour and water have been incorporated into a soft dough. Mix in 2 tablespoons of olive oil. Turn the dough out onto a floured work surface, and knead until the dough is firm but slightly sticky, mixing in more flour if needed. Knead the granulated garlic and Italian seasoning into the dough. (The kneading can be done in a bread machine set on the Dough setting.)

2

Form the dough into a round, and place into an oiled bowl. Brush the top with 1/2 teaspoon of olive oil, cover the bowl with plastic wrap, and allow the dough to rise until double, 1 to 2 hours. Punch down the dough, and cut in half. Form each half into a 12-inch pizza crust, and place on pizza pans.

3

Move a rack to the bottom position in oven, and preheat oven to 450 degrees F (230 degrees C).

4

Bake the pizza crusts on the bottom rack just until firm, 3 to 7 minutes. Allow the crusts to cool for about 10 minutes before topping with sauce, cheese, or other desired ingredients and returning to oven to bake.

NUTRITION FACTS:

139 calories; protein 3.4g; carbohydrates 24.7g; fat 2.8g; sodium 244.1mg.

SPICY SLIDERS

Prep:
30 mins
Cook:
10 mins
Total:
40 mins
Servings:
8
Yield:
8 sliders

INGREDIENTS:

1 ¼ pounds ground beef
1 tablespoon chili powder
2 teaspoons garlic powder
1 jalapeno chile, seeded and finely chopped
1 tablespoon lemon juice
8 slider buns, toasted
1 cup shredded cabbage
½ teaspoon salt
½ teaspoon ground cumin
4 slices Cheddar cheese, halved
1 ½ cups cilantro leaves
½ cup mayonnaise

DIRECTIONS:

1
Heat an outdoor grill to medium-high heat
(375 to 450 degrees F (190 to 230 degrees C).

2
Mix together ground beef, chili powder,
garlic powder, salt, and cumin in a large bowl.
Form into 8 patties. Lightly oil grill grate,
then grill patties until browned,
about 3 minutes per side.
Top with cheese during last minute of grilling.

3
Puree cilantro, mayonnaise,
jalapeno,
and lemon juice in a food
processor or blender.
Spread mixture on bottom half of buns.
Top with cabbage,
patties, and bun tops.

NUTRITION FACTS:

375 calories; protein 18.2g; carbohydrates 160.7g; fat 25.9g;

MEATLOAF MUFFINS WITH OATS

Servings:
12
Yield:
12 meatloaf muffins

INGREDIENTS:

1 tablespoon Worcestershire sauce
½ teaspoon minced garlic
½ teaspoon salt
¼ teaspoon ground black pepper
1 tablespoon ketchup, or as needed (Optional)
3 slices bacon, or as needed (Optional)
1 teaspoon olive oil, or as needed
¾ cup chopped onion
¼ cup chopped green bell pepper
1 pound ground turkey
½ pound mild bulk pork sausage
¾ cup rolled oats
½ cup ketchup (Optional)
¼ cup finely chopped carrot
1 egg, slightly beaten

DIRECTIONS:

1
Preheat the oven to 350 degrees F
(175 degrees C).
Lightly grease a 12-cup muffin tin.

2
Heat oil in a skillet over medium-high heat.
Saute onion and bell pepper in the hot oil until softened,
5 to 7 minutes. Remove from heat and let cool slightly,
about 10 minutes.

3
Combine sauteed onion mixture, turkey,
sausage, oats, 1/2 cup ketchup, carrot, egg,
Worcestershire sauce, garlic,
salt, and pepper in a large bowl.
Mix lightly and thoroughly.

4
Spoon mixture evenly into
the prepared muffin tin using an ice cream scoop,
filling each to the top, mounding if necessary.
Top each with a drizzle of ketchup
and about 1/5 slice of bacon.

5
Bake in the preheated oven until muffins
are browned on tops and no longer pink in the centers,
about 30 minutes.

NUTRITION FACTS:

163 calories; protein 12.4g; carbohydrates 8.2g; fat 9g;

LEMON AND CILANTRO SHRIMP

Prep:
15 mins
Cook:
5 mins
Total:
20 mins
Servings:
4
Yield:
4 servings

INGREDIENTS:

20 jumbo shrimp, peeled and deveined
6 lemons, zested
2 cups chopped fresh cilantro
¼ cup extra virgin olive oil
salt to taste
1 lemon, juiced
ground black pepper to taste

DIRECTIONS:

1
In a bowl, toss shrimp with lemon zest and cilantro to coat.

2
Heat the oil in a skillet over medium heat.
Sprinkle oil with salt, then stir in the shrimp,
lemon zest, and cilantro.
Cook, stirring, 5 minutes,
or until shrimp are opaque.
Transfer to a serving bowl, drizzle with remaining oil,
lemon zest, and olive oil from the skillet.
Squeeze lemon juice over shrimp,
season with pepper, and serve immediately.

NUTRITION FACTS:

278 calories; protein 29.6g; carbohydrates 5.5g; fat 15.7g;

SESAME-ROASTED SALMON

Prep:
10 mins
Cook:
10 mins
Total:
20 mins
Servings:
4
Yield:
4 servings

INGREDIENTS:

cooking spray
2 cloves garlic, minced
2 teaspoons soy sauce
2 teaspoons Dijon mustard
2 teaspoons honey
1 ¼ pounds skin-on salmon fillet, cut into 4 pieces
1 tablespoon black sesame seeds

DIRECTIONS:

1
Preheat oven to 400 degrees F (200 degrees C). Line a baking sheet with aluminum foil and spray with cooking spray.

2
Combine garlic, soy sauce, Dijon mustard, and honey in a bowl. Place salmon, skin-side down, onto the prepared baking sheet. Prick salmon several times with a fork. Spread garlic mixture over salmon; top with sesame seeds.

3
Bake in the preheated oven until fish flakes easily with a fork, 10 to 20 minutes.

NUTRITION FACTS:

232 calories; protein 28.8g; carbohydrates 4.8g; fat 10.2g;

GRILLED POTATO SALAD

Prep:
15 mins
Cook:
30 mins
Additional:
10 mins
Total:
55 mins
Servings:
8

INGREDIENTS:

Original recipe yields 8 servings
Ingredient Checklist
2 pounds red potatoes
2 tablespoons extra-virgin olive oil

Dressing:

½ cup extra-virgin olive oil
1 tablespoon apple cider vinegar
1 teaspoon kosher salt
1 teaspoon ground black pepper
1 clove garlic, chopped
½ teaspoon white sugar
6 slices cooked bacon, chopped
4 green onions, chopped
2 tablespoons minced fresh parsley

DIRECTIONS:

1
Preheat grill for medium heat
and lightly oil the grate.

2
Place potatoes in a bowl;
add 2 tablespoons olive oil and toss to coat.

3
Cook on preheated grill until tender,
about 30 minutes. Cool potatoes,
10 to 15 minutes; cut into quarters.

4
Whisk 1/2 cup olive oil,
vinegar, salt, black pepper,
garlic, and sugar together in a bowl until dressing is smooth.
Toss potatoes, bacon, green onions,
and parsley with dressing
in a bowl until evenly coated.

NUTRITION FACTS:

290 calories; protein 5.7g; carbohydrates 19.4g; fat 21.3g;

GRILLED COD

Prep:
10 mins
Cook:
10 mins
Additional:
15 mins
Total:
35 mins
Servings:
4
Yield:
4 servings

INGREDIENTS:

2 tablespoons butter
1 lemon, juiced
2 tablespoons chopped green onion (white part only)
2 (8 ounce) fillets cod, cut in half
1 tablespoon Cajun seasoning
½ teaspoon lemon pepper
¼ teaspoon salt
¼ teaspoon ground black pepper

DIRECTIONS:

1

Stack about 15 charcoal briquettes
into a grill in a pyramid shape.
If desired, drizzle coals lightly
with lighter fluid and allow to soak
for 1 minute before lighting coals with a match.
Allow fire to spread to all coals, about 10 minutes,
before spreading briquettes out into the grill;
let coals burn until a thin layer of white
ash covers the coals. Lightly oil the grates.

2

Season both sides of cod with Cajun seasoning,
lemon pepper, salt, and black pepper.
Set fish aside on a plate.
Heat butter in a small saucepan over medium heat,
stir in lemon juice and green onion,
and cook until onion is softened, about 3 minutes.

3

Place cod onto oiled grates
and grill until fish is browned and flakes easily,
about 3 minutes per side;
baste with butter mixture frequently while grilling.
Allow cod to rest off the heat
for about 5 minutes before serving.

NUTRITION FACTS:

152 calories; protein 20.3g; carbohydrates 2.2g; fat 6.6g;

OYSTERS ROCKEFELLER

Prep:
30 mins
Cook:
30 mins
Total:
1 hr
Servings:
6
Yield:
24 oysters

INGREDIENTS:

2 slices bacon
24 unopened, fresh, live medium oysters
1 ½ cups cooked spinach
⅓ cup bread crumbs
¼ cup chopped green onions
1 tablespoon chopped fresh parsley
½ teaspoon salt
1 dash hot pepper sauce
3 tablespoons extra virgin olive oil
1 teaspoon anise flavored liqueur
4 cups kosher salt

DIRECTIONS:

1
Preheat oven to 450 degrees F (220 degrees C).
Place bacon in a large, deep skillet.
Cook over medium high heat until evenly brown.
Drain, crumble and set aside.

2
Clean oysters and place in a large stockpot.
Pour in enough water to cover oysters;
bring the water and oysters to a boil.
Remove from heat and drain and cool oysters.
When cooled break the top shell off of each oyster.

3
Using a food processor, chop the bacon, spinach,
bread crumbs, green onions, and parsley.
Add the salt, hot sauce,
olive oil and anise-flavored liqueur
and process until finely chopped but not pureed,
about 10 seconds.

4
Arrange the oysters
in their half shells on a pan with kosher salt.
Spoon some of the spinach mixture on each oyster.
Bake 10 minutes until cooked through,
then change the oven's setting
to broil and broil until browned on top. Serve hot.

NUTRITION FACTS:

148 calories; protein 9.3g; carbohydrates 7.7g; fat 8.9g;

CHAPTER 4:

DESSERT

RECIPES

LEMON CREAM PIE BARS

Prep:
15 mins
Cook:
35 mins
Additional:
2 hrs 30 mins
Total:
3 hrs 20 mins
Servings:
24
Yield:
24 bars

INGREDIENTS:

Crust:

1 ½ cups all-purpose flour
¾ cup canola oil
⅔ cup confectioners' sugar

Filling:

1 (14 ounce) can sweetened condensed milk
3 eggs
½ cup lemon juice
⅓ cup white sugar
1 lemon, zested
¼ teaspoon baking powder

DIRECTIONS:

1
Preheat the oven to 350 degrees F (175 degrees C).

2
Combine flour, oil, and sugar in a bowl. Pat into a 9x13-inch baking pan.

3
Bake in the preheated oven until golden around the edges, about 20 minutes. Cool on a wire rack.

4
Meanwhile, beat sweetened condensed milk, eggs, lemon juice, sugar, lemon zest, and baking powder together until just blended. Pour over the cooled crust.

5
Return to the oven and bake until the filling is set, 13 to 17 minutes. Cool on a wire rack.

6
Refrigerate for at least 2 hours before cutting into 24 bars.

NUTRITION FACTS:

174 calories; protein 2.8g; carbohydrates 21.4g; fat 9g;

FANTASTIC STRUFOLI

Servings:
8
Yield:
8 servings

INGREDIENTS:

1 tablespoon lemon zest
1 ½ cups honey
¾ cup pine nuts
2 ¼ ounces colored candy sprinkles
3 cups all-purpose flour
4 eggs, beaten
¼ cup butter
½ cup white sugar
½ teaspoon salt
2 teaspoons baking powder

DIRECTIONS:

1

Melt the butter or margarine over low heat.
Mix together in a large bowl 2-1/2 cups of the flour.
Add sugar, baking powder,
lemon rind and salt.
Make a depression in the middle.
Drop into it the eggs and the melted butter or margarine.
Mix with a wooden spoon and then
with the hands until dough leaves the sides of the bowl.
Add remaining 1/2 cup of flour as needed.
Knead dough on floured surface
until it isn't sticky anymore.

2

Break off pieces of dough and roll into ropes about the size of a pencil.
Cut into pieces 1/4 inch long.
Roll these pieces into little balls and set aside.

3

In deep frying pan, heat oil about 2 inches deep.
Fry balls until golden brown. Drain on paper towels.

4

In a large saucepan over medium heat,
bring 1-1/2 cups of pure honey to a boil. Let honey boil gently for about 3 minutes before
adding little dough balls, stirring gently with wooden spoon until they are well-coated.

5

Remove balls from honey with a slotted spoon and
place in a deep dish or mound them on a platter.
Sprinkle surface
evenly with nuts and multicolored sprinkles. Cool.

NUTRITION FACTS:

610 calories; protein 11.4g; carbohydrates 108.8g; fat 16.7g;

SICILIAN CANNOLI

Prep:
35 mins
Cook:
10 mins
Additional:
3 hrs 45 mins

INGREDIENTS:

Filling:

2 pounds sheep's milk ricotta cheese
1 ½ cups confectioners' sugar
¼ cup mixed peel
1 ½ ounces dark chocolate, finely chopped

Cannoli Shells:

1 ¼ cups all-purpose flour
3 tablespoons dry Marsala wine, or more to taste
1 tablespoon butter, softened
1 tablespoon white sugar
2 teaspoons vinegar, or more to taste
corn oil for frying

Topping:

3 tablespoons chopped pistachio nuts
2 tablespoons confectioners' sugar, or to taste

DIRECTIONS:

1
Beat ricotta cheese and 1 1/2 cup confectioners' sugar together in a bowl until smooth. Stir in mixed peel and chocolate. Cover and refrigerate for 3 hours.

2
Mix flour, Marsala wine, butter, sugar, and vinegar together in a bowl to make cannoli dough. Wrap in plastic wrap; let rest for 30 minutes.

3
Knead dough on a lightly floured work surface until smooth. Roll to 1/8-inch thickness. Cut into twenty 4-inch squares. Wrap each square around a metal tubular mold, overlapping ends and dabbing with warm water to seal.

4
Heat oil in a large saucepan over medium-high heat. Lower some cannoli molds into the hot oil; cook until shells are golden and crisp, about 10 minutes. Drain on paper towels. Repeat with remaining cannoli molds. Cool briefly; twist molds carefully to remove shells. Let shells cool completely, about 15 minutes.

5
Fill cooled cannoli shells with ricotta filling using a spoon or piping bag. Arrange cannoli on a serving platter. Garnish with pistachios; sprinkle 2 tablespoons confectioners' sugar on top.

NUTRITION FACTS:

177 calories; protein 6.6g; carbohydrates 25.2g; fat 5.5g

PANNA COTTA

Prep:
5 mins
Cook:
10 mins
Additional:
4 hrs
Total:
4 hrs 15 mins
Servings:
6
Yield:
6 servings

INGREDIENTS:

⅓ cup skim milk
1 (.25 ounce) envelope unflavored gelatin
2 ½ cups heavy cream
½ cup white sugar
1 ½ teaspoons vanilla extract

DIRECTIONS:

1

Pour milk into a small bowl,
and stir in the gelatin powder. Set aside.

2

In a saucepan, stir together the heavy cream and sugar,
and set over medium heat. Bring to a full boil, watching carefully,
as the cream will quickly rise to the top of the pan.
Pour the gelatin and milk into the cream,
stirring until completely dissolved.
Cook for one minute, stirring constantly.
Remove from heat, stir in the vanilla
and pour into six individual ramekin dishes.

3

Cool the ramekins uncovered at room temperature.
When cool, cover with plastic wrap, and refrigerate for at least 4 hours, but preferably overnight before serving.

LEMON PUDDING CAKE

Prep:
20 mins
Cook:
40 mins
Total:
1 hr
Servings:
8
Yield:
1 - 8 inch square pan

INGREDIENTS:

¾ cup white sugar
1 pinch salt
3 tablespoons butter, melted
¼ cup sifted all-purpose flour
1 teaspoon grated lemon zest
¼ cup lemon juice
1 ½ cups milk
3 egg yolks
3 egg whites

DIRECTIONS:

1

Preheat oven to 350 degrees F (175 degrees C).
Grease and flour an 8 inch square pan.

2

In a large bowl, combine sugar, salt and melted butter.
Beat in the flour. Stir in the lemon zest and lemon juice.
Combine milk and egg yolks, and add to lemon mixture.

3

In a large glass or metal mixing bowl,
beat egg whites until stiff peaks form.
Fold 1/3 of the whites into the batter,
then quickly fold in remaining
whites until no streaks remain.
Pour batter into prepared pan.

4

Set cake pan in a water bath.
Bake in the preheated oven for 40 minutes,
or until top is lightly browned. Serve warm or cold.

NUTRITION FACTS:

176 calories; protein 4.3g; carbohydrates 24.9g; fat 6.9g

www.ingramcontent.com/pod-product-compliance
Lightning Source LLC
Chambersburg PA
CBHW070931080526
44589CB00013B/1469